WHAT MAKES AMERICA GREAT?

WHAT
MAKES
AMERICA GREAT?

BY

W. EARL WALDROP

The Bethany Press
St. Louis, Mo.

DEDICATION TO THE BOOK

This book is dedicated to Louise and Virginia, my wife and my daughter, who have kept me happy through the years with their love and understanding.

PREFACE

The subject of citizenship has been a passion with the author throughout his ministry. He has spoken out for freedom every time the opportunity has presented itself, and has admonished others to do the same. It is his conviction that the freedom which our nation enjoys today stems from the fact that our founding fathers recognized a living God as the supreme factor and force in the universe, and in the affairs of men and nations.

Since the Awards Juries of the Freedoms Foundation, Valley Forge, Pennsylvania, has singled out the author for the past seven years for his "Speaking Up For Freedom," and one of these years declared the author to be the one minister in the United States of America contributing most to the American way of life through his profession of preaching, it seemed fitting that he follow the suggestion of many friends and put into print some of these preachments.

The chapters which make up this book were first delivered in sermon or lecture form by the author. Two of the chapters were delivered to the congregation of the Park Avenue Christian Church in New York City. The other chapters were delivered in sermon form to the congregation of Central Christian Church of San Antonio, Texas, where it is the author's privilege to serve as the preaching minister;

7

and in lecture forms in numerous civic and patriotic organizations in the Southwest. While the form of the presentations has been changed to conform more to the printed page than to the spoken word, no one who reads these pages will be duped for a moment into thinking they are chapters instead of lectures or sermons. Because they were first delivered in spoken form, there are some facts which are repeated throughout the book. It is the author's belief that these principles are worthy of repeating.

The author is indebted to many sources for some of the contents of these chapters. No attempt at individual credit is made because it is not known to whom such credit is due. Most of the sources have been read and stored in the mind's picture gallery of the author through the years, and have come bubbling up with the overflow of inspiration as he has sat at his desk in meditation and thought.

W. EARL WALDROP, D.D.

San Antonio, Texas

CONTENTS

CHAPTER 1

What's Right with America?

From the beginning our founding fathers built
upon the foundation of great ideals.

LOYAL Americans, irrespective of the administration in office, can conscientiously blend voices with millions of others in singing praises for "the land of the free and the home of the brave."

We all recognize weaknesses in our government and wish that they might be converted into strength. We also admit that many of the obvious weaknesses could be corrected if we as individuals would exert the proper example as citizens. America is as strong as its individuals and the government no stronger than the governed.

Believing as we do that America is the greatest nation in the world, let us seriously consider what makes America great. When we measure greatness we are prone to point to tangible things and say, "These are what make America great." Is it a fair measure of greatness?

Is America great because of her vast land area? Russia covers one-sixth of the world's land area, and China is one-third larger than America. Therefore, we must look beyond physical measurements to discover wherein lies America's greatness.

Is America great because of her large population? We boast of more than 160,000,000 people within the confines of the United States. China can boast of 465,000,000 population and Russia has 212,000,000. Thus we must look beyond a large population for America's greatness.

What about America's military forces? Is this what makes her the greatest nation on earth? When we compare her military strength with that of Russia and China, America is challenged.

Then what does make America great? Is it her productive capacity? Is it her natural resources? Is it her beauty? Is it because she is in control of atomic and hydrogen energy? How much do any of these contribute to America's greatness?

America is great because of her ideals. From the beginning, our ancestors built upon the foundation of great ideals. On July 4, 1776, the Declaration of Independence was adopted by the Continental Congress in Philadelphia. The principles on which America would depend were stated in this document.

> We hold these truths to be self-evident, that all men are created equal, that they are endowed by their Creator with certain unalienable Rights, that among these are Life, Liberty, and the pursuit of Happiness.—That to secure these rights, Governments are instituted among Men, deriving their just powers from the consent of the governed. . . .

On September 17, 1787, the original Constitution of the United States was adopted. And again in this definitive document other ideals were stated which were intended to strengthen the original foundation. The Preamble to the Constitution states:

> We, the people of the United States, in order to form a more perfect Union, establish justice, insure domestic tranquility, provide for the common defence, promote the general welfare, and secure the blessings of liberty to ourselves and our posterity, do ordain and establish this Constitution. . . .

That our land may continue as the greatest nation in the world, let us review a few of the ideals that have made America great.

"We hold these truths to be self-evident, that all men are created equal. . . ." Equality before God and man is one ideal that was woven into the very warp and woof of our country. It was the hope of our founding fathers that every individual who came to live upon these shores would be looked upon by every other citizen as a person, equal before God and man.

What a noble concept! Have we lived up to this ideal one hundred per cent? This ideal has been lost many times by some American citizens. There was a time when some of God's children were owned in slavery and were denied equal rights. Even today many citizens of minority races are discriminated against. Because of the sensitivity of some of our citizens we are approaching this ideal as never before. Slowly, but surely, the scales of social justice are coming to a better balance.

Why has this ideal not been accomplished in its entirety? Is it because you and I, while demanding equality for ourselves, have failed to guarantee the same privilege to others? What about you? Are you proud of your conduct in the field of social relations? Most of us are not. When you and I can truthfully say, "I hold these truths to be self-evident, that all men are created equal . . . ," then America will become in deed and in truth the "Land of the free."

"We hold these truths to be self-evident, that all men are . . . endowed by their Creator with certain unalienable Rights, that among these are Life, Liberty, and the pursuit of Happiness." Have we lived up to this ideal one hundred per cent? No, every day in America someone goes hungry. Every day in America many die for lack of care and attention. There are still those in our country who do not possess these inalienable rights. But we are nearer the goal than ever before.

No word in the English language is prized more highly than is the word "liberty," or freedom. To preserve and defend this inalienable right, governments have been overthrown, wars have been fought, and the blood of humanity shed. Ask any citizen what he prizes most about the American way of life. Most will answer "Freedom" without hesitation. It is a prize worth having, but let us not forget that freedom is for everyone; if we value freedom for ourselves, we must be willing to grant it to others.

Second only to freedom, and not really second, because it is a fruit of freedom, is "the pursuit of happiness." Happiness is a state of being that every individual in the world pursues. . . . It was in the minds of our founding fathers that every individual must have the right to pursue and to achieve happiness. The late Franklin Delano Roosevelt knew well the quality of happiness our fathers had in their minds when he set forth his four freedoms: freedom from want, freedom from fear, freedom of worship, and freedom of speech. This is certainly a noble pursuit, but we must not make it a selfish one. If happiness is one of man's inalienable rights, then it is for all or none. America will continue to be the greatest nation in the world only as we turn from our selfish pursuits and simulations of personal happiness, and look each to the other's happiness and welfare. We must learn to include the pronouns, "we," "us," and "ours," or we will perish.

Another ideal that has made America great and which undergirds all the others is the ideal of religion. Abraham Lincoln, speaking of the "new birth of freedom," insisted that it should and must be "under God." With Lincoln, as with others, this ideal has stimulated Americans from the signers of the Mayflower Compact to the Constitution and to our present day.

At one of the stormy sessions of the Constitutional Convention, Benjamin Franklin, then in his eighty-first year, arose and addressed that body in these memorable words:

> I have lived, sir, a long time, and the longer I live, the more convincing proofs I see of this truth: That God *governs in the affairs of men.* And if a sparrow cannot fall to the ground without His notice, is it possible that an empire can rise without His aid?
>
> We have been assured, sir, in the sacred writings, that "except the Lord build the House, they labour in vain that built it." I firmly believe this; and I

also believe that without His concurring aid we shall succeed in this political building no better than the builders of Babel.

Indeed all of the ideals we have mentioned, the marks of America's greatness, were inspired by Almighty God. If America continues to be the greatest nation in the world, her citizens must continue to be God-fearing. When Jesus told the Pharisees and Herodians to "Render therefore to Caesar the things that are Caesar's, and to God the things that are God's" (Matt. 22:21), he inseparably linked man's citizenship with his religion. One cannot be a good Christian without being a good citizen and vice versa.

To develop in America the recognition that all men are created equal is a high motive, but it is not enough. To develop in America a guarantee to the rights of life is not enough. To create in this great country a guarantee of, and a love for, liberty and freedom is not enough. If we have all these, and exclude God, America will collapse. Of course we all love to sing:

My country! 'tis of thee, Sweet land of Liberty,
Of thee I sing;
Land where my fathers died! Land of the pilgrims' pride!
From every mountain side let freedom ring.

But let us also be ready and willing to sing with all our hearts:

Our fathers' God! to Thee, Author of liberty,
To Thee we sing:
Long may our land be bright with freedom's holy light;
Protect us by Thy might, Great God, our King!

17

If we remember that

Unless the LORD watches over the city,
   the watchman stays awake in vain

                      (Psalm 127:1), and

Righteousness exalts a nation,
     but sin is a reproach to any people

                          (Proverbs 14:34)

then we will continue to build and to perpetuate "the land of the free and the home of the brave."

A few years ago a fast train running between New York and San Francisco had a wreck. Before the accident occurred the man who told this story was sitting in a club car talking with a famous surgeon. In the confusion that followed the derailment, they were separated. Remembering this doctor, the man ran in search of him to minister to two people who appeared to need medical attention. Finally, in the maze of wreckage and confusion, the doctor was found and rushed to the wounded. After an examination the surgeon raised his head and said: "This man needs an operation at once or he will die. Here I am, a doctor who could save his life, but I'm on vacation. I left my instruments at home."

Many Americans are on vacation from citizenship today. America must have the loyalty of every citizen to remain great. Every American ought to exert his Christian love, his spirit of brotherhood, and his spirit of tolerance, if he prizes freedom. Let's keep America great!

CHAPTER 2

Why Believe in America?

It is the right of every citizen in America
to claim and pursue equality of opportunity.

WHEN one is privileged to live in as great a country as the United States of America, he ought to believe in it strongly and know why he so believes. Often the philosophy that has made this country is taken for granted, and thereby endangered. If one will study the philosophy of the Bible, the Mayflower Compact, the Declaration of Independence, and the Constitution, he cannot help being thrilled that he is a part of such a strong heritage. He cannot help seeing that these philosophies continue as the measure of her greatness.

A firm faith in God was the foundation upon which our nation was laid. When the Pilgrims landed at Plymouth Rock, their first act on these shores was to hold a service of thanksgiving and to ask God's guidance on their venture in the new world. God was present not only at our beginning, but he has been present also during the years of our development.

During the Constitutional Convention, when America was trying to come of age, after six weeks of wrangling to no avail, George Washington arose and said to the colonial delegates: "There can be no government without morality, there can be no morality without religion, and there can be no religion without God." Thus did the father of our country remind the architects of American democracy that God must be at the center of life in this nation.

When we reflect on this statement of Washington, we need not be surprised that the Preamble to the Constitution should have been one of the two noblest political documents of all time—the other is the Declaration of Independence. It is also significant that in the Mayflower Compact, the Bill of Rights, the Declaration of Independence, and the Constitution, we find the reality of God recognized many times. The Declaration of Independence begins with the assumption that man is a child of God: "We hold these truths to be self-evident, that all men are created equal, that they are endowed by their Creator with certain unalienable rights. . . . "

When Abraham Lincoln gave his immortal Gettysburg Address, he asked prayerfully that "This nation, under God, shall have a new birth of freedom." We need to get this nation back "under God." We need to strengthen her foundations so that we may continue to have a "new birth of freedom."

One of the guarantees America made to her citizens from the beginning was the freedom to worship God according to the dictates of the individual conscience. The first subject dealt with in the Bill of Rights is freedom of religion. In effect it says, "Congress shall make no law respecting an establishment of religion or prohibiting the free exercise thereof." This principle was dear to our forefathers, and it is equally dear to every American citizen today. Religious intolerance was one of the main reasons why the settlers left Europe. They wanted to get away from suppressed religion and a state church. Shortly after they arrived on these shores, religious intolerance began to crop up in the new land. When the Quakers tried to take their religion with them to Massachusetts, the Puritans persecuted them with floggings, tortures, and hangings. In Virginia no person was allowed to vote unless he was a member of a certain church. As a result of all of this, the Constitution, by its very First Amendment, separated church and state. The principle of freedom of religion must be kept alive in America. Throughout her history America has guaranteed to all citizens their freedom to worship without interference from the state. A demand which we have every right to make of our presidents is that no religious preference be shown, and that no religious body be identified or dignified with diplomatic status. We American citizens must demand protection for freedom to worship God according to the dictates of our own conscience.

Very early in the history of this country our forefathers felt the need of guaranteeing to its citizens the inalienable right of freedom of speech and freedom of worship. Included, therefore, in the First Amendment to the Constitution of the United States is the guarantee to every citizen the freedom of speech and of the press, freedom of expression. Every American citizen deserves this God-given freedom. This assurance is one of the bases of her abiding greatness. It has encouraged people to think through any problems America has faced and work out solutions to them. It has encouraged people to openly criticize the government when it has needed criticism. There are nations in our world where this philosophy is not enjoyed. In Russia and its satellites today, citizens are stripped of individual dignity. The words and even the thoughts of their people are controlled. Thank God for America where any citizen can think, speak, and write freely.

In a country like America, where freedom is everything the word implies, there will always be dangerous decisions and difficult problems. One problem, now prevalent, involves the philosophy of freedom of expression in our American system of separating church and state. While teaching people through its educational institutions to think for themselves, the state, which supports no church, cannot always teach them right ideas. This need not be a threatening danger so long as we all support our churches and keep our homes closely allied with the church. As long as these two institutions combine their resources to teach the youth of our land godly thoughts, we need have no fear for America.

High on the list of reasons for believing in America is freedom of enterprise. While the Constitution of the United States does not mention the freedom of enterprise, several of its provisions point to this inalienable right, including the ownership of private property and the equality of opportunity. To keep self-respect, individual initiative, every person must have the right to own private property: something he can call his own—something he can share with his brother in Christian love. There are nations in our world today where this is denied. The state owns everything and no matter how hard a person works he is permitted to retain only a fraction of the fruits of his efforts. Thank God for the privilege of living in a country that upholds the principle of freedom to our property and the freedom to enjoy the fruits of one's labor.

In a free nation it is the right of every citizen to claim and pursue equality of opportunity. It does not work one hundred per cent, but it can be made to work. It has worked in the past; it continues to function. When we consider that men like Abraham Lincoln, born in a one-room log cabin in the hills of Kentucky, and Dwight D. Eisenhower, born of Mennonite parents in Texas, can become presidents of the United States, we are more than ever aware of the freedom of opportunity in America.

America stands for democracy—a government for the people and by the people. A nation cannot exist without a strong central government. However, government exists for the primary purpose of guaranteeing the inalienable rights herein mentioned, to its individual citizens. The dignity of the individual is just as essential as is the government with all of its agencies. Thank God for democracy; the kind of democracy that has made America great!

Believing in all these things, what are we Americans going to do to preserve them for posterity? It is essential that we realize that the survival of the American way of life depends upon individual integrity and responsibility. As for me, I am going to strengthen my own fundamental faith in God. If these inalienable rights are ever in danger, it will be due in part to the fact that we as citizens have lost our faith in God. The dignity of the individual is tied up with faith in God. When faith in God is lost, so are self-respect and respect for others.

The late Archbishop of Canterbury, William Temple, in his book, *The Hope of a New World,* struck a keynote when he said that the tragedy of our time is due largely to man's omitting God. Furthermore, he said that the solution to our world problems lies in man reclaiming God.

Dr. Homer W. Carpenter, in his volume, *The Future Is Now,* quotes John Temple Graves as saying, "I am not a preacher, I am only a wicked newspaperman, but I am convinced that unless we deepen in our nation a sense of God, all we are doing in the direction of a new world will be futile." Faith in God can most certainly be restored in our nation, if we as individuals restore him in our lives. Moreover, we should promote faith in God on the part of every other citizen. We should resolve to give every other citizen the freedom to worship God in his own way, as we claim that freedom for ourselves. We must realize that personal dignity demands that every person find God in his own way; but realizing also that personal happiness depends on drawing near to God, one should urge all men to turn to him.

Furthermore, we should not misuse the freedom guaranteed to us by the Constitution of the United States, and we should insist that every other citizen of this great nation not misuse it. I have come to realize it is when I misuse freedom that freedom becomes endangered. We individually must take an active part in politics and see to it that others do likewise, in order that this nation under God shall continue to have "a new birth of freedom," and that it shall continue to be a government "of the people, by the people and for the people."

CHAPTER 3

The Christian Idea of Freedom

When we take it upon ourselves to deny freedom in any shape, form, or fashion to another human being, we cease to be free ourselves and become enslaved to selfishness.

F REEDOM needs protection today more than any time since the beginning of the Christian Era. Not only do we need to protect our freedom from nations who have never had such freedom and consequently do not know what it means: we need to redefine freedom, to see it in a Christian reference. What is our conception of freedom? Is it something which we have inherited, and for which we must fight? Is it something which we prize selfishly and do not want to share with anyone? Do we consider our freedom a blessing which we gladly share with all of God's children? We need to answer these questions—we are not good citizens until we have sought out the proper answers to these and other questions about freedom.

Let us take a look at some of the definitions of freedom that are prevalent today. The dictionary defines freedom as exemption from necessity in choice and actions. This definition would enslave most of us to boredom and loneliness instead of bringing freedom. The dictionary further says that freedom is immunity and exemption, for example, freedom from care. But you and I agree that none of us could live happily without cares and responsibilities. Again the dictionary reminds us that freedom is the possession of the rights or privileges of a citizen, as of a city. These definitions are all too shallow. We must pursue our definitions further if we are to learn what freedom really is.

What are some of the definitions of freedom which we hold as precious today? It may be said that freedom gives one the right to do as he pleases without restraints. There again you and I realize that when we are free to do as we please, we soon find that we are not happy with what we have done. Others say that freedom is liberty, and thus affords a license to say and to do what he chooses. These definitions are likewise shallow and do not merit further discussion. But notice if you will that every one of them defines a selfish concept of freedom—my rights, my protection! Notice also that these selfish and shallow definitions do not require any responsibilities on the part of the individual in order to deserve or to justify these freedoms. None of the definitions here mentioned are Christian.

Let us turn to the Christian idea of freedom, and see how different it is from these shallow and selfish definitions. Jesus said, "If you continue in my word, you are truly my disciples, and you will know the truth, and the truth will make you free." (John 8:31-32.) The Christian idea is that real freedom is freedom in the truth. This has been eternally true. It is certainly true from a practical standpoint. It has been proved by man that scientific truth frees us from disease, from superstition, from fear, and from unnecessary toil. Concern for truth in the field of education assures us of freedom from ignorance, provincialism and from small-mindedness. It has been proved by science that mental health stems from the cleansing power of truth: truth about God, truth about the world, and truth about ourselves.

Freedom of speech for the Christian means the right to speak the truth. It does not mean the right to say what one pleases. Freedom of speech actually places one under obligation to speak the eternal truth. The individual who speaks falsely ceases to be free. He becomes a slave to error and to untruth, and he no longer deserves the right to freedom of speech. Freedom to do as one pleases, means to the Christian that he is free to do the will of God, and when he does things counter to God's creation and his will, then he ceases to be free in the truest sense, and becomes a slave to sin and to the forces which seek to destroy the will of God. Freedom to worship God means to the Christian that he is free to exercise that right of worship according to his belief and choice. It does not mean freedom to worship or not to worship. Freedom of religion means freedom for worship and to worship; it can never mean freedom from worship.

The Christian idea of freedom is unselfishness. Paul is the authority for this belief in unselfish freedom. Listen to his words: "For you were called to freedom, brethren; only do not use your freedom as an opportunity for the flesh, but through love be servants of one another." (Galatians 5:13.) When man stands high in the image of God he is least concerned about his own value. But when he ceases to reflect the image of God and begins to reflect his own personal and selfish rights and privileges he is no longer in the image of God.

Let us study the implications Paul makes. First, he says we are free because we were born to be free. God made us free moral agents. He further says that we are most free when we are not enslaved to selfishness. When we take it upon ourselves to deny freedom in any shape, form, or fashion to another human being, we cease to be free ourselves and become enslaved to selfishness. Sometimes those who speak loudest about freedom make the mistake of treating it as personal, like "my privileges" and "my rights," and fail to say anything at all about "my responsibilities." When our founding fathers wrote the Declaration of Independence, they were completely unselfish. Listen to the language of it:

> We hold these truths to be self-evident, that all men
> are created equal, that they are endowed by their
> Creator with certain unalienable rights; that
> among these are Life, Liberty and the pursuit of
> Happiness.

Notice they did not say "We are created equal." Rather they said "All men are created equal." It was their belief that life, liberty, and the pursuit of happiness were God-endowed and were for all. It is as if they were rewriting the words of the Apostle Paul, "through love be servants of one another." The only way to retain freedom is to guarantee it to all. Paul says this in a crisp warning that follows the statment just made. "For the whole law is fulfilled in one word, 'You shall love your neighbor as yourself.' But if you bite and devour one another take heed that you are not consumed by one another." (Galatians 5:14-15.)

Abraham Lincoln recognized this same danger when he said:

> Our reliance is in love of liberty which God has planted in us and our defense is in the spirit which prizes liberty as the heritage of all men in all lands everywhere. Destroy this spirit, and we have planted the seeds of despotism at our own doors. Those who deny freedom to others deserve it not for themselves, and, under a just God, cannot long retain it. This country, with its institutions, belongs to the people who inhabit it. Whenever they shall grow weary of the existing government they can exercise their constitutional right of amending it; or their revolutionary right to dismember and overthrow it. Why should there not be patient confidence in the ultimate justice of the people? Is there any better or equal hope in the world?

How can we best serve and protect our freedom today? Jesus gave the answer. He says that we can best serve and protect freedom by continuing in his word, by seeking always after the truth. What good is freedom unless we have the truth of how to administer it? E. P. Dickie tells the story of a slave-trading vessel which was returning from Africa with its cargo of "black ivory." Two hundred slaves were packed together under the decks. One of them was a great chief, who lay in the hold plotting revenge for this deadly insult. His opportunity came. When the guards had grown careless he overpowered the sailor who had the key for the irons which chained them. Quietly he released the other slaves and at a given signal they rushed on deck, overpowered the crew, murdered them, and threw their bodies overboard. They were free. But there was something they had forgotten. None of them knew anything about sailing a ship. They had seen the sailors watching the compass, but to them the compass was like a god or devil. They thought they might persuade it to guide them home if they fell down and worshiped it. But the compass was useless to them because they knew nothing of the great magnetic forces which the compass obeys. True, the slaves had their freedom and power, but freedom and power without the right direction lead inevitably to disaster.

We can best protect freedom by serving one another in love. Love is the key that unlocks the door of freedom. Love is the supreme declaration out of which the quest for freedom issues, the obedience through which it is secured, and the discipline in which it is perfected. Paul admonishes us "through love be servants of one another." Freedom needs a vision; Christianity offers the way, the truth and the life of Jesus Christ. Freedom needs a controlling temper and a master law; Christianity offers love. Freedom needs a discipline; Christianity offers the constraints of Christian goodness and its own fullness of life. Freedom needs an understanding of the meaning of life and history; Christianity offers the realm of God. Freedom needs its own declaration of independence; Christianity offers the proclamation the centuries have validated; "So if the Son makes you free, you will be free indeed." (John 8:36.)

CHAPTER 4

Why Be Christian?

If our civilization is to survive, it is important—
yes, it is even imperative—that every freethinking person know who he is, what he believes, and why he believes it.

SEVERAL years ago an important public servant arose before a large group of people to speak. His importance in the community had assured him a good audience. Electricity was in the air, as the throng waited in high anticipation for the words that would fall from this man's lips. As he arose, there was a momentary stir in the audience, a thundering applause; then complete silence. As every eye was turned on this man, he began to speak. Staring into the sea of faces, he asked, "Can anyone here tell me who I am?" This man was a sudden victim of amnesia. He had actually forgotten who he was. It is a tragic situation for anyone to be stricken with amnesia. It is even more tragic when millions of people self-inflict themselves with a sort of spiritual amnesia and, to all intents and purposes, forget who they are, what they believe, and why they believe it.

John Ruskin once said every man should constantly ask himself three questions: Who am I? Where am I going? and, What must I do on the way? We are now living in a very critical period of history. If our civilization is to survive, it is important—it is imperative—that every freethinking person know who he is, what he believes, and why he believes it.

Why be Christian? Because the only sensible alternative to communism, the rival philosophy that seeks to control the world today, is Christianity. Not a *laissez-faire* Christianity, but an aggressive, progressive, objective Christianity. Christianity and communism are diametrically opposed to each other. They are now, and for several years have been, in deadly combat. Until recently it has been a cold war—one of words, of propaganda. Communism got the better of this part of the battle because communists crusaded more strenuously for communistic ideals than Christians crusaded for Christian ideals. Only God knows who will win out in the end, should the battle progress into a shooting war. One thing is certain: If we expect to win and save our Christian way of life, we Christians must be willing to live by our ideals, and when necessary die for them.

The time is later than most people think. It is high time that all Americans, especially professing Christians, took stock of their values. Men need to seek out for themselves the answers to such questions as: Who am I? What do I believe? Why do I believe it?

Why be Christian? Because Christianity teaches man that his first allegiance is due the God who created him. Communists do not believe in God. Their religion, communism, teaches them that their first allegiance must be to the "Party."

The fact of the matter is that communism teaches that God is a myth. Dr. John Bennett says that communism is based on the philosophy of dialectical materialism combined with atheism. In itself it is no more atheistic than any other naturalistic philosophy that accepts the experienced world of nature and history as self-sufficient. It is, however, accompanied by a bitter polemic against all theistic religions. But even if there were no antireligious feeling and even if no reasons based upon social experience could be alleged for discrediting all forms of theistic religion, the philosophy has no place for faith in God as Creator on whom the whole world of nature and history depends.

God is the Creator of the world and he has not left his world to run itself or to be run by men. God is the LORD of humanity; the LORD of public affairs as well as of the life of each individual. God as we know him through the Bible is no abstract principle, no far-off deity, but the active Creator and Redeemer of the world, and our Christian life is lived under a command to do the will of God. History has validated the fact that God is with man in history, and that He seeks to deliver men from the many forms of bondage in which they are held; yes, the bondage in which men hold one another. All groups of people are equally the objects of the love and concern of God. If his way could prevail throughout the world, all communities would be conscious of the real welfare of all God's children.

When Moses went up to Mount Sinai to receive the Ten Commandments from God, the children of Israel grew weary of waiting for his return and were afraid. They said to Aaron that he must make them gods to worship. He asked for their jewelry which was molded into an idol in the form of a golden calf. When Moses came down from the mountain and found that the people had corrupted themselves and were worshiping idols, he stood in the gate of the camp and sounded a clarion call to all, "Who is on the LORD's side? Come to me." (Exodus 32:26.) This is the call that must go out from the people of God today. Who is on the Lord's side, let him stand up and be counted! Let him know what he believes and why he believes. Let him accept God as our refuge and our strength.

During the last few years more and more Christians have pledged only a lip service to God. Many who have come to the church on Sunday and looked pious have gone out on Monday to do honor to satanic forces. Let every Christian confess his sin of apathy and stand condemned before God in the firm faith that God gives a second chance. If we will do this, we may gain the strength to make the best of that other chance to gain redemption. This is no time for lip service; it is time for vital action on the part of God's followers.

Why be Christian? Because of what the church has meant to our world. The church as we know it may not be perfect, as God measures perfection, but it is the only institution in the world that constantly preaches and teaches that God's will must be done on earth if we are to attain a perfect society. It is the institution that has nurtured all of us and has leavened the society in which we live with its moral and spiritual principles. When the communist revolution came to Russia, that country turned her back on the church. Many of her churches were made into recreational centers and devoted to other uses. In the Red Square in Moscow hung a placard which read: "Religion, the opiate of the people," thus discrediting all that the church had tried to teach.

Allow the writer this personal confession: I believe the church is the greatest institution on earth. I cannot remember a day when the church was not the dominant influence in my life for good. When I went 10,000 miles from home, during World War II, to the jungles of the Pacific Islands, my church followed me, giving the encouragement necessary to carry on when it seemed physically impossible to go any further. The grammar school and the high school in which I received my early education were, from their inception, church-supported institutions. The colleges in which I received my degrees were church-supported colleges. Even if they had not been directly supported by the church, history tells me that higher education in America is a child of the church. Therefore, most of us owe our education directly and indirectly to the church. When we look around in our home city today, at its social institutions, its orphanages, its civic, altruistic programs, its ideals, we know that all these were originally started and supported by the church.

Of course, the church, as we know it, is not perfect. None of us fulfills the principles of Christ, whose name it bears, one hundred per cent. There have been many times in my own life when I have been envious, laden with pride, burdened with prejudices and ill will. Many people who profess membership in the church as Christians have hate in their hearts against their brothers. Many so-called Christians hold prejudices and antipathies. We must admit that the soil in which communism has grown stems from failure on the part of all Christians to live up to their profession of love for all God's children, as taught by the church. In spite of this, we must agree that the church is the strongest institution we have which can constantly hold up before the world the principles and the judgments of God.

The church is the only institution known to man that can and will eventually bring about a free and peaceful world.

The church holds the answer, if man will follow its direction. The great scientist, the late Albert Einstein, who was driven from his native Germany because of his race, said that when dictator Hitler came to power, Einstein and other German citizens first looked with hope to the educational institutions to rise up and oppose Hitler's barbaric rule. But their hopes were in vain. Next they looked to the various social institutions, and again their hopes were in vain. Then Einstein said they next looked with desperate hope to the church, and there they found the only institution in all of Germany that had the courage to stand up and oppose Hitler to his face, and to openly fight his Nazi programs. That is the kind of church we are talking about.

That is the same kind of church that existed in Norway, when that country was delivered to Hitler and slavery. Consider Bishop Berggrav and his fellow Christians who knelt and prayed in the snow outside their church, when they were denied the use of it by armed guards, and arose to sing, "A mighty fortress is our God, a bulwark never failing." That is the kind of church we are talking about. Wherever that kind of church appears, communism, with all its dialectical materialism, will not have a chance—not even with one third of the world's population, which it influences today.

Why be Christian? Because Christianity teaches honesty and fair play. Communism practices and preaches falsity and intrigue. Why be Christian? Because Christianity holds up the right of every man to own something he can point to with pride and call his own, something he can share with his family and neighbors. Communism teaches the abolition of private property. Why be Christian? Because Christianity teaches that persons, even those who oppose us, are to be respected and loved for their own sake. Communism holds up the revolutionary idea that opponents are obstacles to be removed or neutralized by whatever means. What is hidden behind the many Communist curtains would probably make the rest of the world shudder with righteous indignation.

Let us now come to the crux of the matter. As enemies of communism, in a free and peaceful world in which communism is making some progress with its aggressive and deceptive methods, what can we do about it?

In the first place, we must make our influence felt where it counts most, right at home in our own church. We must give as much energy as we have in making our church stronger, so that its influence can be felt in the social and political life of our community. This is something we can all do. We must advocate and practice the brotherhood of man in our everyday life. We must look upon people of all races as children of God, each deserving the same measure of his blessings. We must not allow our souls to become burdened with prejudices against other religions. We must recognize other faiths who believe in God, and feel that they, too, can be prophetic voices in the wilderness calling men to believe and practice the fatherhood of God and the brotherhood of man, as redemptive factors in the world.

Although we are natural enemies of communism, we must not allow ourselves to hate individuals who are Communists. Like all people, they are children of God who, by consent or by circumstance, have become victims of a dictatorial political system that has enslaved them body and soul. It is our duty as Christians to help them; to work constantly to free them from their bondage, that they too may know the blessedness of peace and freedom.

The principal weapons of communism are false doctrines, fed in alluring guises to uninformed and unthinking persons in the form of glittering, but vain, promises. Boiled down to one word this means propaganda, and the Communist is incredibly adept at wielding this weapon. Free America likewise possesses powerful weapons—peace, liberty, and righteousness. Here in America we make an issue of maintaining our freedom—because we want to be free. If we can awaken in the hearts and minds of the people of the Soviet countries the wish and the resolve to be free, then we will have made real progress toward emancipating these captives of communism. If these people are ever to believe and have confidence in their own future, then they must have constant assurance that all people who enjoy peace and liberty and righteousness are their friends.

We as a people or as a rich and powerful nation should not attempt to convert other peoples of the world to our way of life by luring them with gold. It is a well-known and long-established fact that love, friendship, and loyalty cannot be bought. Neither should we feel that we must ultimately have a fighting war with communism; that we must subdue the Communist people on the battlefield before we can have peace, liberty, and righteousness throughout the world. The only war we want to wage is a war of ideals, and the ultimate goal of this World War is to have the peoples of all nations enjoy the blessings of freedom. The most potent force in this war of ideals is spiritual, and the most decisive factor is a holy cause, and all Christians must be willing to join hands unselfishly and risk everything, that we might extend these benefits to all God's children, thus realizing the vision of Isaiah:

nation shall not lift up sword against nation,
    neither shall they learn war any more.   (Isaiah 2:4.)

CHAPTER 5

Spiritual Foundations for Peace

Our foundation for peace on earth must be laid
in the hearts of individuals.

Is peace possible? What causes war? Who won the wars of history? What are the spiritual foundations for peace?

As we face the future from here, we are reminded of some of the disappointments of the past. During our generation "The War to Make the World Safe for Democracy," better known as World War I, was fought. Only a short time ago another most destructive war came to an end. It was known as World War II, or "The War to End All Wars." Less than five years after World War II, our nation was drawn into another conflict which started in Korea, and in which there were more than 140,000 American casualties before fighting stopped. We and our Allies were acclaimed the victors of World War I and World War II. Yes, we defeated the enemy, but we lost far more than we gained. In wars there are no winners; everyone loses. Our dear ones—the individuals who make up our nation—paid a mighty price for our alleged victories. Flash a few pictures on your mind's screen so as to bring home to you the fact that in war even victory is costly.

Picture a group of men crouched in foxholes. They have been there, in the same holes, for five days. A foxhole can get mighty filthy and uncomfortable if you have to live in it for five days without getting out. Finally word came that it was safe to crawl out and make way back to the rear area for rest and recuperation. They were happy men; they had visions of a hot meal, cigarettes, coffee. The business of easing back was slow. Before reaching their destination enemy bombers came over and dropped some bombs; many of them never got back. Yes, in war even victory is costly.

Picture a young Air Force pilot from Pennsylvania who was within one mission of being sent back to the States for home duty. At the open-air theater the night before his last mission, home seemed in sight. The next evening the announcement came that Charles did not come back. He was shot down over Wewak in New Guinea. Yes, in war even victory is costly.

Picture a group of men sitting on the ground with mess kits in hand, eating their evening meal of C-rations. The battle of Leyte in the Philippines was over except for an air raid once in a while, which the men had learned to take in stride. All seemed peaceful and quiet on that fateful evening; there was no alert. Suddenly, out of nowhere an enemy bomb came and fell in the midst of the men as they were eating. After it was over, eighty purple hearts were given out; forty-three of them posthumously. Yes, war is a costly business, heartbreakingly costly.

Go with me to one of the general hospitals in the Dutch East Indies and see row upon row of hospital beds occupied by men who had returned from the front. In the first bed is a man with both arms and both eyes gone. Next to him is a man with both arms shot off. Next is a man with one arm and one leg missing. Next is one paralyzed from his hips down with no hope of ever walking again. True, it isn't a pretty picture, but it is proof that war is not only costly, it is a hellish business.

These are only a few pictures, but they will suffice to convince every good American that we must work and pray that our nation may never be engaged in another war. We must earnestly seek knowledge and direction for the whole world, which will outlaw and make impossible another war. As a free nation let every American citizen earnestly pray for those who must make world decisions, that we may have a world wherein dwell righteousness, peace, and equality for all.

Peace does not mean the mere absence of war. Peace is a way of life, and before it can be made world-wide, spiritual foundations must be laid in the hearts of individuals. In his book, *Night Unto Night,* Philip Wylie said that peace is not the prerequisite of nations. The peace of the world will come only when the people who comprise it have found inner peace. The Apostle Paul said the same thing centuries ago: "Let each man take care how he builds . . . For no other foundation can anyone lay than that which is laid, which is Jesus Christ." (1 Corinthians 3:10-11.)

Disputes between national governments play a part in starting wars, but the individual citizen makes up these nations that create and agitate the dissensions which result in war. Therefore, it is in the hearts of individuals that we must lay our foundation for peace on earth. If the human element fails, then all has failed. Character in individual lives is the greatest bulwark the world can build against war.

The great wall of China was an impregnable structure when it was finished; it seemed a superb way to gain security. However, within a few years of its completion the enemy had breached it three times. It was breached, not by breaking down the wall, but by bribing the gatekeepers. The human element had failed. What collapsed was character, not the great structure men had constructed with their hands. As a nation we need to take cognizance of this fact today.

Political intrigues do not make for world peace. The building of war machines—larger armies, more planes, more ships, and more atomic and hydrogen weapons—keeps nations poised for war. More than anything else today we need to be building character on the foundation of Jesus the Christ. Nations may build giant political structures, large air forces, and armies and navies, but if we as individual citizens fail to build in our hearts the love of God, then all of these giant preparations, made by our nation with peaceful intent, will surely crumble and fall. It is the human element that we must make strong. If we are to have a peaceful world, we must build human character on the foundation of the humility of Christ.

Hitler started World War II because of racial pride and prejudice. He inculcated into the hearts of the German people the idea that they were a super race, better and stronger than all other races of the world. His ambitions to conquer the world were built on the foundation of pride and prejudice. Peace in the world cannot be built on a foundation of pride and prejudice; if these foundations are laid in the hearts of people, as in the case of Hitler, war will be the inevitable result. This is the exact opposite of the teachings and examples

47

of Jesus. We ought to know by now that pride and prejudice are poor foundations on which to build. But have we learned our lesson sufficiently?

The Korean War and the war in Indochina were both started by the Communists, and were caused by class pride and prejudice. The Communist Manifesto declares that the world belongs to the proletariat; that only the working classes of people have any rights and privileges. This is exactly opposite to the teachings of Jesus, who declared that the world belongs to God. The capitalist system of government is prone to say the world belongs to those who have money enough to buy it. This is likewise exactly opposite to the teachings of our Lord.

Pride and prejudice are fruits of ignorance, and no race or nationality has a monopoly on ignorance. It is obvious, therefore, that our problem is truly world-wide. Some sections of our American nation are presently dealing with the problem of whether or not certain races should be segregated. Here again we come face to face with that bad element which Hitler so eloquently taught the German nation before he led them onto the battlefield to conquer the world—*racial pride and prejudice*. These are times when we must hold and exercise great faith and courage. It is the writer's sincere feeling that our American nation will never succumb to any type of upheaval or encounter based upon racial distinction or class hatred among its people. We love our freedom and we have profited from Hitler's experience. Let every good American citizen, without distinction as to race, creed, or color, work together as a nation for peace and justice at home and throughout the world—a peace which we as a free Christian people can build on the foundation of the humility of Jesus the Christ.

Peace can never be built on the foundations of cynicism and skepticism; they will not sustain peace. The insincerity of skepticism and cynicism is tremendously magnified when we reverse things and try to imagine a world of peace and brotherhood built on anti-Christ thinking. When we think of a world built on the premise that there is no God, at once we are reminded of the parable of Jesus concerning a man who built his house on the sand, only to see it fall when the storms came. If you are ever tempted to surrender your Christian ideals, all you have to do is take cognizance of the company you would be joining: Hitler, Mussolini, Stalin, others who have preceded them, and their henchmen of to-day who seek to destroy the free forces of the world.

We need to value the principles of Jesus Christ to build a world of righteousness. We must pattern our individual characters after the Prince of Peace if we are to have a world of peace. These are times that call for firm faith in God, and for courage to stand up and be counted. Unless we build on this foundation, our efforts are in vain.

We must build on the foundation of the love of Christ. Surely we have seen that we cannot build a world of peace and brotherhood on the foundation of hate and ill will. These things bring war instead of peace. Hate creates disunity. Love creates unity and brotherhood. Hate causes us to forget and disregard the rights of others. Love causes us to look upon the rights of others with the same view that we take of our own rights and privileges.

What is love? It is hard to define. When one seeks to put love into words he finds that words are insufficient to describe it. What is love? The writer knows of a man who threw himself on a hand grenade to keep its explosion from killing and wounding his buddies. That is love. What is love? There was a Man who while hanging on the cross looked down upon his tormentors and said, "Father, forgive them; for they know not what they do." (Luke 23:34.) This is the kind of love we need in our lives today if we are to build a peaceful world. We must begin by building the foundations of love.

"Love your enemies" was the hardest of all the imperatives of Jesus. Man will always be restless until he is actually showing good will toward his enemies. Loving the unlovely is the most difficult thing man has to do, but it must become a reality before there can be peace on earth. Herbert Hoover has said that we can have peace or we can have revenge, but we cannot have both.

Yes, the spiritual foundations for peace are humility, faith, courage, and love. Whether or not these become a reality in our world depends on whether or not you and I allow them to become realities in our lives. Do we really want peace in our world? If we do, we can have it. But if we are to have it, we must build on the foundations of Jesus Christ. "For no other foundation can anyone lay than that which is laid, which is Jesus Christ." (1 Corinthians 3:11.)

CHAPTER 6

What Makes A Good Citizen?

In America the idea of good citizenship was born, and it has grown up under the basic conviction that God is the supreme ruler of life.

WHAT makes a good citizen? It is true, of course, that one who is born in the United States of American parents is classified a natural-born citizen of the country. But the mere fact of birth does not make one a good citizen. A foreign-born person may become a citizen of our country when he fulfills certain legal requirements. The mere fulfillment of the legal conditions of naturalization does not make a good citizen. To be a good citizen we must conform to certain basic fundamentals as well as contribute to society.

A fundamental belief in God is unquestionably the first basic requirement for good citizenship. When asked what he considered the greatest commandment, Jesus said: "You shall love the Lord your God with all your heart, and with all your soul, and with all your mind." (Matthew 22:37.) Being a good citizen is synonymous with being our best spiritually.

It is not our occupation, or social standing, or what we own, that makes us a good citizen; it is our ideals. Ideals are the fruits of our convictions. In America the idea of good citizenship was born, and it has grown up under the basic conviction that God is the supreme ruler of life.

The basic belief among great Americans has always been that when we attain faith in God, there are set in motion in our life certain ideals that affect our every act. When we attain faith in God, there is set in motion in our life a love that grows warmer as our faith becomes stronger. When faith weakens, then love grows cold. When we attain a great faith in God, there grows in our life a genuine concern for others. When faith grows weak, this concern for others lessens. When we have a firm faith in God, there comes into our life a respect for authority in the realms of both spirit and law. When faith grows weak, this respect for authority weakens.

William Jennings Bryan uttered a cardinal belief of Americans in a speech at the 1896 Democratic Convention, when he said that the humblest citizen of all the land, clad in the armor of a righteous cause, is stronger than all the hosts of error. When one is clad in the armor of faith in God, he has fulfilled the first requirement of a good citizen. If you would be a good citizen of your nation, then you must also be a good citizen of the kingdom of God. Faith in God is essential to good citizenship.

A second requirement of good citizenship is a proper balance between rights and responsibilities. We speak glibly about our rights as citizens, and we can be justly proud of them. But until we have seen to it that these rights carry with them some of the great responsibilities which face our nation, then we have not begun to be good citizens. The right to worship God in our own way without interference from the state is wonderful. When we consider the price and the sacrifices paid by our founding fathers for this freedom, we are challenged. Here is a right that no good citizen would want to relinquish. It is undoubtedly a God-given right, and we should never permit anyone to take it away from us. Yet, this God-given right is endangered when we fail to accept the responsibilities that go with it. If we interpret this to mean that we may worship or we may not worship as we see fit, then we endanger this freedom for ourselves and for every other person. The fact that we have this inalienable right certainly puts us under obligation to exercise it as good citizens. Every time I stay away from the worship service of my church, I am guilty of misusing the freedom to worship God according to the dictates of my own conscience.

The right to free speech which we enjoy here in America is indeed a great blessing. There are other places in our world today where people do not enjoy either free worship or free speech. In such places they have to be very careful what they say and who hears them say it. We live in a nation where we can freely say what we wish to say. How wonderful is this right to free speech. Yet, if this right is to be preserved and protected, we should feel an obligation always to speak carefully and correctly. We are under obligation to speak truthfully, and we should not dare misuse this freedom by speaking falsely. If we use the right of free speech to broadcast error and false propaganda, then most certainly we will hasten the day when this blessing will not be a reality for any of us. To be a good citizen we must use this freedom of speech to spread the truth. Jesus said, "And you will know the truth, and the truth will make you free." (John 8:32.) Therefore, we cannot be good Christians or good citizens unless we use this right of free speech intelligently.

The right to have and to enjoy the privacy of our homes is another blessing that we of this great nation all hold near and dear. Our national government guarantees this basic right to us, but not without grave responsibilities on the part of every citizen. To be guaranteed freedom in our homes requires us to maintain our homes in the best form. The fact that here in America we enjoy unrestricted freedom, combined with privacy in the home, does not give us the license to organize Communist cells or other organizations which are hostile and dangerous to our American way of life. Neither does it give us the license to misuse these freedoms in any other way. The sacred freedoms which are assured every American home automatically place upon each and every one the responsibility to see that high moral and ethical standards are practiced.

The unrestricted right to bargain for and to own private property is another freedom which we in America do enjoy, and of which we can be proud. This and other freedoms do not exist in some nations, perhaps because the citizens of those nations have not accepted all of the prerequisites and related responsibilities which go with good citizenship. If we are to remain a free and independent nation, then we must be willing at all times to accept all the responsibilities which our freedoms place upon us; and we must dedicate a reasonable share of our efforts and our possessions to maintain the church, community, and government. To do otherwise would be to misuse our God-given freedoms.

Daniel Webster once declared that whatever makes men good Christians makes them good citizens. This is another way of saying that we must render to both God and country their just dues. Each day of life we are made to realize that our religion and citizenship are very closely akin, and in both areas of life we need to pray earnestly and continuously for divine guidance and direction.

Another requirement of good citizenship is that we share its fruits with others. This is likewise true in the realm of religion, which reminds me of an old saying, "There are only two things you can do with the Christian faith—give it away or give it up." And when applied to the idea of good citizenship it simply means this: if we keep it, we lose it; if we share it, we possess it forever.

Good citizenship requires that we serve others in public service. Jean Jacques Rousseau wrote in his book, *The Social Contract,* book I, chapter 4, that as soon as public service ceases to be the chief business of a citizen, the state is not far from its fall. Jesus said something akin to this when speaking to his disciples: "He who is greatest among you shall be your servant; whoever exalts himself will be humbled, and whoever humbles himself will be exalted." (Matthew 23:11-12.)

What is a good citizen? He is one who not only believes firmly in his country; he believes in God. He is one who has a proper balance between rights and responsibilities. He is one who shares the fruits of good citizenship with his fellow men. The way to solve many of the problems faced by our nation and our people today is to approach them from the spiritual point of view. A spiritual sickness demands a spiritual cure. As Herbert Hoover said, "Our strength is not in politics, in prices, in production, or in price controls. Our strength lies in spiritual concepts."

CHAPTER 7

Citizenship and Vocation

Are you using your talents to their maximum for
the glory of God through serving humanity?

ANY discussion of citizenship should include vocation. We must recognize that there are many facets to vocation. Before any individual can approximate good citizenship, he must examine his own life in the light of his vocation as a child of God. There are three basic facts which should be considered in this discussion: First, God calls every individual to some work. Second, since God calls, vocation becomes a divine and sacred responsibility. Third, talents are God-given and should therefore be used to make the world a better place in which his children can live abundantly.

One of the first things the writer remembers learning about the church was that God calls preachers. That fact made an indelible impression on his young mind, and alerted him for the call when it came. Had he not been so alerted the chances are he might not have heard the summons.

As great and important as this call is in the world, it is the writer's firm belief that the church has made a mistake in stressing the calling of the preacher, while utterly neglecting to teach that God also calls bankers, truck drivers, doctors, and lawyers. It is a dangerous mistake because it has a tendency to departmentalize life and to set man's religious life apart from the rest of his life.

God calls each of us to some task in his great scheme of things. We must cease putting religion into a pigeonhole, thus making it a department of life. It is dangerous for one to be a lodge member one night of the week, luncheon clubber one day at noon; a businessman during the week, and a so-called Christian on Sunday. It just won't work! Unless a man lets his Christian principles and his Christian zeal leaven the other activities of his life, he is missing the mark as far as Christianity is concerned.

When Jesus called his disciples, he went to the business circles of life to find them. He chose men who were already active in a gainful pursuit. Some of them continued in their vocation and used it as a means of spreading the gospel. We have every reason to believe that Paul continued his occupation after accepting the call of his Lord. Many of his original disciples stayed with their work.

Whatever your occupation it will not glorify God unless it glorifies man. Therefore, your work must be honorable or it will discredit you as a good citizen. Use your every opportunity to glorify God and serve his children through your life work, and you will be a partner of Him who created you. And what is more, all of this will make you a good citizen.

We have looked too long upon vocation merely as a means of earning a living. In the home, in the school, and in the institutions of higher learning, we have taught our children to equate success with security and comforts with contributions. We have failed to see that this is only one facet to vocation. This is only one result, and a natural one, of giving ourselves to some calling.

Choosing a vocation should begin with a realization of the needs of the world. Every young person before selecting a career should look around him and evaluate his talents in the light of the world's needs. There are many suffering who need to be healed. There are many ignorant who need to be taught. There are many hungry who need to be fed. There are many sorrowing who need to be comforted. There are many for whom the meaning of life has slipped from their grasp. They need to be shown the way. There are many dishonest areas of political activity that need the leavening of some Christian statesman. There are many areas in the business world that need to be touched by the spirit of some Christlike man. Let the young person look around at these needs and determine where he can serve best. Let him ask God in what capacity he can be used. Then, when he gets the answer, let him prepare for that work and go where he can do the most good in that capacity. Every man ought to pursue that vocation through which his life can count for Christ.

If there is one who is dissatisfied with his vocation, or who has reason to be ashamed of it, let him be assured that it is not too late to change. It is never too late. Albert Schweitzer changed his vocation to that of a medical missionary after he had become accomplished in three other fields. He looked at the needs of the African natives and decided that he should go there and help lift the health standards of those people. He went with a Christian motive and therefore through his vocation as a Christian physician has perhaps done more than any other individual to lift the standards of Christian principles in all of the world.

What about the man who has never felt that he was called to any particular task, but who seems happy and satisfied that he is making a contribution? Let him be assured that God has called him. Sometimes he calls and we answer without realizing that we have had a divine visitation. Every man is called of God. Let every man answer that call and give of his best, certain that his vocation is sacred.

Let every child of God face the fact that talents are God-given and should therefore be used to make God's world a better world. Every individual is endowed with some peculiar talent that is best fitted to him. Not every man could be a surgeon with deft hands to perform tedious operations. Not every woman could have the patience and fortitude to be a nurse with a special touch that seems to put new life into the sick body. Not every man could be an accountant and know how to deal successfully with financial and mathematical problems. Not every individual could be a lawyer with a mind for giving legal advice and the eloquence to plead cases before the courts of our land. All of us know individuals who possess these and many other peculiar talents. How do you suppose it happens that one man can make heavenly music on a violin, while a great surgeon cannot carry a tune or play a musical instrument? It doesn't just happen that way. God has made us so that each one will have a different but individual vocation.

Our talents place us under responsibility to use them to the glory of God and his children. Surely this is what Jesus was teaching in his parable of the talents. The lesson is clear that man must use his talents or they will be taken away from him. To the two servants who invested their talents the master gave his blessings. But to the one who refused to invest it, he gave a curse, and took it away from him.

What are your talents? What is your vocation? You must answer to yourself and to your God. Inventory your life and find out what your talents are. Then ask yourself if you are using them to their maximum production for the glory of God through serving humanity. Then ask God how you can invest them for greater returns. See your work as a window through which the divine light can shine in a peculiar way.

It is good to be a church worker. It is good to have one's shoulder to the wheel of God's church in some capacity. The greatest need in our world today is not greater and larger church organizations. On the contrary, the greatest need is for more people who belong to the church to take the spirit of God that they find in the church and distribute it through their relationships every day in the week. In other words we need more Christian citizens.

Dr. Elton Trueblood in his book, *The Common Ventures of Life,* says that Christianity lives or dies, not by what goes on in the churches, but by what goes on outside of them. He means, of course, that if a man comes to church to get filled with the spirit of God, and then does not go out and share that spirit with others, his coming was for naught. It is through our work that we become an influence for God's kingdom. If we do not let our light shine there, it might as well not shine anywhere. If a man will not practice Christianity in his daily toil, then he will not practice it anywhere.

It bears repeating that citizenship and Christianity are very closely tied up with vocation. Good citizenship requires that we use our talents and powers for the good of our society. Each of us should pray the prayer of the Psalmist every day:

> . . . establish thou the work of our hands upon us, yea, the work of our hands establish thou it. (Psalm 90:17.)

CHAPTER 8

Citizenship
and
Man's Relationships

We live in a highly literate age, but we are
ignorant in the area of life that counts most.
We still do not know how to live with one
another in Christian love.

CITIZENSHIP is at its best when human relations are at their highest. Life stands or falls on the relationships of human beings. The coming of the kingdom of God depends on how people get along with each other. It is in this realm that we are guilty of illiteracy. We live in a highly literate age. We know much about many things. Through science we have conquered most of the fatal diseases that once ravaged mankind. Through education we have raised the level of culture and literacy in the world. Through historical criticism we have learned more about the Bible than ever before. Through the science of aviation man has learned to fly in space at supersonic speeds, and therefore brought every part of the world into closer proximity. And now, through the science of nuclear fission, we have learned to split the atom and harness atomic energy. Yes, with all this literacy we are still illiterate in the area of life that counts most. We still do not know how to live with one another in Christian love.

Jesus has a message for us that we need to learn before our citizenship is complete. "This is my commandment, that you love one another as I have loved you." (John 15:12.) In the Gospel of Matthew he says:

> "For if you love those who love you, what reward have you? Do not even the tax collectors do the same? And if you salute only your brethren, what more are you doing than others? Do not even the Gentiles do the same? You, therefore, must be perfect, as your heavenly Father is perfect." (Matt. 5:46-48.)

Jesus lays it on our hearts to set the example of love. If Christians do not set the example, who will?

If citizenship is to be courageously Christian we must do more than salute across the lines of religious divisions. Jesus would say to us today, If you salute only those who hold your opinions, what reward have you? Do not even the pagans do this? If human relations cannot be their best in this realm, how can we expect them to be the best in the other realms of life? One of the sins of Christ's church is its divisions. Jesus prayed with the disciples "that they may all be one." (John 17:21.) When we consider these words and then realize that there are three hundred Protestant divisions in Christendom, we know we have yet to answer the prayer of our Lord for unity. We have failed in our Christian love. No wonder we have been unable to convince the world that God sent his Son to save the world.

We continue to send missionaries to foreign fields to save the pagans, presenting a divided Christ. Some have presented a Methodist Christ, some a Presbyterian Christ and some a Baptist. No wonder we have confused rather than helped those who need Christ.

The classic story of the three churches on opposite corners in a certain town is still in a measure true today. On one corner was a Baptist church; on another a Methodist church; and on the third corner stood a Christian church. A man passing through the town during services heard the choirs of all three churches singing at once. The Baptist choir was singing, "Will there be any stars in my crown?"; the Methodist choir was singing, "No, Not One"; while the Christian choir was singing with gusto, "O That Will Be Glory for Me."

The writer's own church, the brotherhood of the Disciples of Christ, has had as its plea through the years the unity of the church. But there have been those who interpreted this plea to mean that all other religious bodies should lose their identity and come join Disciples of Christ. This has been the selfish plea of all communions. One of the slogans of Disciples of Christ has been "In essentials, unity; in opinions, liberty; in all things, charity." Most of the things that keep our divisions prevalent are opinions, not essentials. God speed the day when all religious bodies can say, "We are ready to lose our identity as a division of Christianity; we are willing to be swallowed up in the church universal."

The stage has been set in a sort of federal union that we call a Council of Churches, but we still have a long way to go. In San Antonio, Texas, there are two hundred seventy churches representing Protestantism. Of this number only one hundred will co-operate in our council of churches. The others are going their own individual ways.

Is there any doubt what Christ meant when he prayed, "that they may all be one"? God help us to see and recognize that ours is a common pilgrimage in search of one God. Those who wrote the Bible were content, for the most part, with telling a story. When Stephen and Paul were asked to justify their faith, they gave the record and let it rest: He brought us out of Egypt against dreadful odds; he took us through the wilderness when we could not help ourselves; he led us into the promised land; he brought forth a savior, who lived, died, and rose again. The revelation, they held, was in what had occurred, and never primarily in doctrines and opinions. Christianity is not merely a way of life, not a speculation, but a reaction to a series of historical facts. The heart of the gospel is the exciting news that the eternal Word became flesh and dwelt among men. Why don't we agree on that and let our faith begin with that fact? If Christianity is to win out over the pagan and godless ideologies that are loose in the world today, it will win only as it presents a united front in the name of Christ. We need some bigger and better salutes across the lines of religious divisions!

We need some bigger and better salutes across the picket fence of nations. The international situation which confronts the world today is caused by a breakdown of human relations. Citizenship has not been at its best. We need to listen to Jesus as he says, "If you love only those of your own nation, what reward have you?" Let us face some realistic facts. Communism continues to take over large slices of the world. Asia, the greatest land area and the largest population mass in the world, is going over to communism. The white rule in Asia is over. How and why has this come about? It is because we have misunderstood human relations on the international level. While Asia has been starving for food and other necessities, we have tried to force on them American democracy and the American way of life before they were ready for it. When they have cried out for food, we have offered them the right to vote. Communism has deceivingly offered these people bread and land, and a hungry man will always take bread before he will take the right to vote, especially when he does not understand what free elections mean.

Where we have given physical assistance in the Point Four program, we have continued to look upon the nationals as inferior people and have called them "gooks" and "grease balls." We have not extended our hands and recognized them as children of God and therefore brothers.

If we had spent $50,000,000,000 to provide bread and the love of Christ to the needy of the world, instead of arms and ammunition to protect ourselves, communism would not be so widespread. We have jockeyed ourselves into the position where the best idea is being defeated by the worst idea.

The world needs bigger and better salutes across these and other lines of division if the growing world conflict is to be relieved. Those people in the world today who recognize the nature of our problems are all saying that Christ is the answer. Christian citizenship must become a reality. General Douglas MacArthur, standing on the deck of the battleship "Missouri" at the Japanese surrender, said, "The problem now resolves itself into a theological one." Dr. George A. Buttrick, an eminent American preacher, has said that it is Christ or chaos. Dr. Frank C. Laubach, that great religious leader of the world, has said that survival or suicide hangs on the fine thread of whether or not we choose to be Christian.

Do you ask, "What has all this got to do with me?" It has everything to do with you. Human relations stand or fall on how one man loves another and gets along with him. If we cannot love one another in the home, in the church, across religious differences, political differences, and across racial lines, how can we love those who are foreign to us and whom we do not know?

Let us look at the chain reaction of society. The home depends on how the people who live in it get along with each other and love one another. The church depends on how people love one another and work with each other. The racial situation in America looks for a solution to how we respond to the love of Christ and his command to love our brethren. The world situation then finds its solution not confined to the conference table but dependent on the love of one man for another.

Focus your attention once more on the words of Jesus:

"This is my commandment, that you love one another." (John 15:12.) Is there any doubt what Christ is telling us to do? The command is to flavor all of our human relations with the spirit of Christ; the promise is that if we do this, our reward will be a peaceful world, and a peaceful heart. Both are prizes worthy of our life's work. God help us to become more literate in these realms of human relations.

CHAPTER 9

The Power of Written Words

What individuals and groups read and believe
determines their destiny.

THE writer has recently examined two books that are familiar to almost everyone. These books are both nicely bound, they are about the same size and contain approximately the same number of pages. Neither of them was written in English; both were originally published in another language and were later translated into English. Both books contain words of power, but actually when one commences to read them, the only similarity is in outward appearance. Perhaps no two books could be more dissimilar.

One of these books, titled by its author *Mein Kampf,* translated into English, "My Fight," was written by a dictator who had delusions of ruling the world with an iron fist. Where his book was read and its principles practiced, freedom did not exist; racial hatreds and prejudices were developed. Where this book was read and its principles practiced, great armies were trained to do the bidding of tyrants; minorities had no chance of free expression. Where this book was read and its principles practiced, war, with all its hell and destruction, resulted. Where this book was read and its principles practiced, eventual dishonor and annihilation have come. Yes, Adolf Hitler intended that his book *Mein Kampf* be a book of power.

The other book examined is known the world over as the Holy Bible. This book was written by many authors. As a matter of fact, we cannot be certain who wrote many of the books contained in the Bible. The Bible is a book of transforming power. Where this book is read and its principles practiced, ignorance and illiteracy are gradually overcome. Where this book is read and its principles practiced, the hungry are fed, the naked clothed, and the thirsty are given the water of life. Where this book is read and its principles practiced, love takes the place of hate, and souls lost in darkness and dishonor find their way to the land of pure delight. Where this book is read and its principles practiced, broken hearts are mended, lonely hearts are refreshed, and troubled minds find peace. This book has proved to be what one of its authors said it was, "A lamp to my feet and a light to my path." (Psalm 119:105.) This illustration exemplifies the power of the printed page.

Printed words can be more dangerous than bullets. If their stolidity is believed, masses are frequently moved to inhumane controversies. On the other hand, the right printed words can be most helpful to every individual who reads and believes them.

Dr. Royal J. Dye tells the story of a missionary in Africa who was trying to teach a native to read. The native was superstitious and would not accept writing as a means of expression. To prove his point the missionary wrote a message on a piece of paper and told the native if he would take the paper to his wife in the village she would give him a dozen oranges. He offered the written message to the native, but the native would not accept it; if the paper could talk it could also bite. Finally the native split a stick and held out the cleft end for the missionary to slip the paper in, and off he went to the village. When he reached the missionary's wife, he handed the paper to her and she walked in the house reading it aloud. When she came out with the dozen oranges, she saw two black heels running down the jungle trail. Trembling fascination and curiosity had broken down into superstitious terror. The native felt sure that this magic was too powerful to be safe.

We can smile at the African native, but we need to see with him the danger of printed words, if wrong words. History validates the fact that people become what they read and believe. The things an individual reads shape his everyday thinking, and very often the things an individual reads determine his actions. By the same reasoning, the things which a group of individuals can be persuaded to read and believe, shape their actions, and thus determine the life of a nation.

When the German people were persuaded to read and believe ideals set forth in *Mein Kampf,* the entire German nation lost her head, and in the end lost her life and standing in the family of nations. When only a few of the Roman Empire were persuaded to read the word of God and abide by his teachings, a nation was able to throw off the yoke of dictatorship. Yes, written words have power—the power to impart good information or bad information. Abraham Lincoln once said to Dennis Hanks, "The things I want to know are in books. My best friend is the man who'll give me a good book I ain't read." There is so much that we all need to know, which we can get only from books. Every person, who prizes the freedom inherent in democracy, should read often the Declaration of Independence, and the Bill of Rights.

There is much secular information which we need if we are to be good citizens. To face the problems that are prevalent today without knowing what has happened to others in similar circumstances, is like going into a strange play in the middle of the second act, expecting to get the benefit of the whole show. It is my firm belief that if one is to be prepared to live at his best, he must know what has gone before in this drama we call life. At some time everyone should read H. G. Wells's *Outline of History,* and Whitaker's *We Cannot Escape History.* Every good citizen must keep abreast with current news—both local and world-wide. This is not the chore that it used to be. Modern media of communication have facilitated the dissemination of news and information. The problem is to separate the good from the bad; to be able to recognize propaganda when it is substituted for facts.

But secular information is not enough. Good citizenship demands that we also read for the purpose of gaining religious information. In addition to reading the Bible, every Protestant Christian should also read an interdenominational publication titled *The Christian Century.* There are many religious books which we ought to read in order to become better informed about our religion and about religious problems. The greatest and most valuable source of religious information is found in the Bible.

When Paul said to Timothy, "Do your best to present yourself to God as one approved, a workman who has no need to be ashamed, rightly handling the word of truth" (2 Timothy 2:15), he was admonishing him to read the sacred scrolls, which corresponded to our Bible. We cannot live up to our best as Christians unless we familiarize ourselves with the information and knowledge contained in the New Testament. Problems of life are here discussed and ultimate answers can be found. Every one of us is faced constantly with problems of temptation and sin. The Bible contains information that we need to know concerning the problems of suffering, those of our everyday life. The Bible contains information concerning the problems not only of life, but also of salvation. There are certain things man must do if he is to be saved from the hell of uselessness. The Bible offers a way of immortality to all those who can interpret and apply its exhortations.

Written words have the power to impart inspiration as well as information. Mere information is not sufficient unless we become inspired with what we read. There is much in the secular world about which we need to become concerned, if we are to be useful citizens. Written words cannot have the power of inspiration in our lives unless we read with the right motive. Francis Bacon once said that we must read not only to contradict and confute, nor to believe and take for granted, nor to find talk and discourse, but also that we might weigh and consider.

When we read about the United Nations, from the right motive, we cannot help but be inspired about what it is trying to accomplish in the world. When we read about the political conditions of our nation today, from the right perspective, we cannot help wanting to have a part in politics. When people became inspired about the writings of John Greenleaf Whittier, the abolition of slavery became a reality in our world. When people became inspired about the things that poured forth from the pen of John Howard, prison reforms became a reality. Thus we need to become inspired about many things in the secular press today if we are to preserve democracy and the freedoms it affords.

Many books have therapeutic value. A few years ago while convalescing, I read a volume that contributed greatly to my recovery. The book was written by Betsey Barton, who ten years before had met with an accident which left her paralyzed from the waist down. It was the story of one who had sought and found divine help to face life as a partial invalid. The title of the book was *And Now to Live Again*. It inspired me to rise above self-pity because of affliction and fight to gain my mental and spiritual equilibrium.

William Lyons Phelps once said that his convictions on individual liberty, which changed the entire course of his life, were born in his soul while reading John Stuart Mills's *Essay on Liberty*. Many of you could undoubtedly add your own personal experiences to these mentioned of how your life has been changed through the inspiration of written words. The greatest power of inspiration comes from the words written on the pages of the Bible. Throughout the ages countless men and women have been inspired to do seemingly impossible things by reading and studying the Bible. We have all found that to read the Bible for information also gives us inspiration.

Some are guilty of reading the Bible just enough to have their eyes opened to the reality of Christ, but not enough to have their vision focused on him as their Savior. There are some who have read the Bible just enough to come in contact with Christ, but not sufficiently to gain inspiration. Many have had just enough contact with him through the pages of the Bible to make them decent but not enough to make them dynamically Christian.

Paul reminds us that if we are to be approved of God, we must study the Bible. Few can really study the life of Christ without becoming so inspired that they will want to follow in the Savior's footsteps. When we see the face of Christ in the word pictures of the New Testament, we become inspired to give him our all, just like the young man who gazed into the face of Christ in a painting and exclaimed: "That man Christ Jesus can have all of me."

Everyone ought to read for the inspiration of his soul. We cannot read the life of our Lord and his teachings without sensing the large amount of reading he did while on earth. We know that he read philosophy and the sacred writings for he quoted from them profusely. He quoted from the philosophy of Confucius and Buddha, as well as the philosophies of Islam and Judaism. Many of the teachings of Jesus were taken from these sources, and stated by him positively. The golden rule is to be found in all four of the sources just mentioned; but Jesus was the only one who stated it positively. If our Lord felt the need of reading for information and inspiration, how much more then should we, his followers, feel the need. If we wish to be better citizens and finer Christians, we must turn with reverence and discerning appreciation to the written word.

CHAPTER 10

Christ and Your Citizenship

To be a good citizen of any nation one must likewise be a good citizen of the kingdom of God.

NEVER has there been a time when citizenship needed to be stressed as it does today. It needs to be rethought and re-evaluated. There is no better way to do this than to permit Christ and his spirit to guide us in that re-evaluation.

Jesus gave us an insight into his evaluation of citizenship; it is recorded for us in the Bible. A group of Pharisees came to him with a question which they hoped would make him betray himself politically. They asked him whether or not it was lawful, from a religious point of view, to pay taxes to Caesar. His answer was a challenge to them and to us. He asked them to bring a coin. Holding the coin before him, he asked whose picture was on it. They answered that it was Caesar's. Then he directed to them this challenging statement: "Render therefore to Caesar the things that are Caesar's, and to God the things that are God's." (Matthew 22:21.) In this statement our Lord says to the Pharisees and to us that to be a good citizen of any nation, one must also be a good citizen of the kingdom of God. Loyalty to God and loyalty to one's country are prerequisites of good citizenship.

The words "good citizenship" no longer have the high meaning they once had. They have been exploited in many ways and by many people in our generation. Something has happened to us. We have seen rulers, leaders, and statesmen in high places refuse to recognize our living God as the supreme factor and force in the universe, and in the lives of men and the affairs of nations. We have seen men high in the leadership of our own nation turn out to be traitors to their country. Spies have been found in our midst. Our armies have been weakened from within by the selfish action of men in high places. Most of us have had the opportunity to watch so-called American citizens join in parades and other movements, advocating things inimical to our own free and independent nation.

Let us not throw too many stones at those whom we can single out until we have checked our own citizenship. There are a few questions we should ask ourselves before becoming too self-righteous. Let us ask ourselves, What have I done to make my country better? Have I taken an active part in government, or have I said, "Leave it to the professional politicians"? Because of my own inactivity, have I made it possible for the wicked and dishonest to gain entrance into my government? To these and other similar questions most of us would have to say, "Yes, I am guilty. I have failed to live up to the requirements of a good citizen." Most of us have failed to render to both Caesar and to God their just dues. Through inactivity and lethargy we have cheapened the meaning of good citizenship both in our nation and in the kingdom of God. Jesus intimates in the Scriptures that to be a good citizen we must be loyal to both God and country. Listen to his words again, "Render, therefore, to Caesar the things that are Caesar's and to God the things that are God's."

In our kind of world and in our kind of nation what does it mean to render to Caesar the things that are Caesar's? In our democratic form of government, "of the people, for the people and by the people," it means that we must take part in selecting our public servants. It is the duty of every good citizen to fulfill that requirement. We should all be grateful for citizenship in a nation where opposing factions can vie for office, and where we have freedom to worship as we choose and to vote however we please. There are nations on this earth where people do not enjoy free worship and where they must go to the polls at the point of a gun; and under such conditions there is no choice. The existence of dictatorships, or corruption in governments, abuses of power, and the acceptance of things which stand for evil, can always be singled out as positive proof that somewhere along the line an alarming number of citizens have relaxed their standards and their vigilance. It is my duty and your duty as good citizens to vote to uphold and perpetuate the system of free elections so that it may continue to be the God-given right of every citizen of this nation to be proud he is an American.

In our kind of free and independent nation one must also share in the expenses of government if he is to be a good citizen. Although it is the right of every citizen to complain about high taxes and make just criticism of our government, it is also the duty of every citizen to have a part in paying the bills. When any American begins to cheat on his tax obligations, trying to dodge his responsibility of sharing the expenses of government, he is wrong in thus shirking his responsibility as a good citizen.

To be a good citizen and to render to Caesar the things that are Caesar's, we must obey the laws of our nation.

Let us turn now and ask what it means to render to God the things that are God's. If, in order to be a good citizen of our nation, we must also be good citizens of the kingdom of God, we ought to know what we are expected to render to God. According to the teachings of Jesus, if we are to be worthy citizens of the kingdom of God, we must obey the laws of God. Many of these laws were written by Moses: You shall not kill, commit adultery, steal, lie, covet, and so forth. Jesus said all of these could be stated in two laws: You shall love God, and you shall love your fellow men. If love for God and love for man is at the root of our life, the rest of the laws will be obeyed automatically.

It is made plain for us in Holy Writ that to be a good citizen of the kingdom of God, we must support the church, which is God's institution on earth to bring about his kingdom here as it is in heaven. It is the consensus of opinion of the biblical writers of the New Testament that no person can be his best unless he attends the services of the church; unless he shares in the expenses of the church; and unless he gives his life as well as his treasures to God. Jesus was talking to persons, yes, to you and to me, when he said, "Render therefore to Caesar the things that are Caesar's, and to God the things that are God's." (Matthew 22:21.)

We need a revolution in America today. Do not say "Amen," until you hear what it takes to bring it about. You are the person to bring it about. Does someone ask, "But what can I do? What can one person do to bring about a revolution?" Each one can bring about a one-man revolution, a revolution within himself.

Consider some facts about yourself: you are not duplicated anywhere in the world. Of the fingerprints of the more than 160,000,000 people in the United States, no two are alike. Yours is different from every other one. God is not a celestial machine that turns out replicas. He is a divine craftsman who makes individuals. So you, being the only one like you in the human story, are essential in God's great scheme of things. When you or I fail, it is worse than one note on a piano missing. Your witness is unique. Therefore, you can let Christ come into your life, and bring about a revolution. If this can happen to your life, lethargy will be replaced by active citizenship. Prejudice will be replaced by brotherhood. Hate will be replaced by love. You will cease asking, How much can I get out of the government? You will in turn begin to ask, How much can I give to the government?

A national revolution must begin with individuals. As far as you are concerned, there can be no revolution until it begins in you. There are many things you can do toward becoming a better citizen of your country and in the kingdom of God. The one thing that you can do is to vote. Whenever an election nears, a familiar slogan reminds you that it doesn't make any difference how you vote, so long as you vote. You must be prepared to vote intelligently. Learn as much as you can about the platforms of all political parties, and of all candidates in every election. After you have this information, ask which party can best lead our nation in the troublous times through which we are passing. Then pray; ask God to guide you in making your decision. Do this no matter if your mind is already made up. If you follow these simple instructions, you will be fulfilling in part the requirements of a good citizen and a good Christian. And what is more, you will be helping to preserve our American freedom, and our great Christian traditions.

"Render therefore to Caesar the things that are Caesar's, and to God the things that are God's." (Matthew 22:21.) Give your best to your nation and to your God.

CHAPTER 11

Let Freedom Ring

We must be as willing to guarantee our
inalienable rights to others as we are
to enjoy them ourselves.

WHEN Samuel F. Smith wrote the words, "My Country, 'Tis of Thee," he ended the first stanza with these words, "From every mountain side, let freedom ring!" The only difficulty with this beautiful ending is that freedom does not ring from every mountain side. Freedom rings from the hearts and lives of persons who have achieved it. Freedom is not impersonal, it is personal. Freedom is not tangible, it is spiritual.

The Apostle Paul was saying that freedom is personal and spiritual when he wrote to the Christians at Galatia, "For freedom Christ has set us free; stand fast therefore, and do not submit again to a yoke of slavery." (Galatians 5:1.) "For you were called to freedom, brethren; only do not use your freedom as an opportunity for the flesh, but through love be servants of one another." (Galatians 5:13.) It will be profitable for us to review our definitions of freedom, and to come to some conclusions as to how we can achieve true freedom, and protect that freedom which others have earned for us.

As Americans we are guaranteed under the Constitution of the United States many freedoms. Among them are: freedom of life, of liberty, and of the pursuit of happiness;

freedom of speech, of press, and of public assembly; freedom of worship and religion; freedom of choice of profession and occupation; freedom to acquire, possess, and inherit property; freedom in the establishment and maintenance of free enterprise and the possession and enjoyment of the fruits of one's labor; freedom of participation in the selection of elective government officials, and the right to aspire to public office, and freedom in the use of the ballot.

These freedoms are prized highly by all of us. As we think of them and enumerate them, we sing with real feeling, "Let freedom ring." But, what do we mean when we say it? What is the real meaning of freedom?

Does freedom mean that we are at liberty to do as we please? There are millions of people in America, who, when they assert their faith in freedom, mean to say that they believe that it is man's natural right to do just exactly as he pleases under all circumstances. These will point to the fact that American freedom was won once and for all at Bunker Hill and Valley Forge and Yorktown; that men left their bloody footprints in the snow, winning their cause against an empire, and that is that. They will name the statesmen who secured this freedom which has supplied the outstanding example of the triumphant march of democracy through the years. They will point out to you also that because of the above-mentioned facts persons have the right to individual initiative and actions with a minimum of interference from the state. That may be the freedom of the Liberty League and economic individualism, but it is not a true definition of freedom.

Because of this current definition of freedom, it needs to be rethought. It is too noble a word to be bandied around and misused. It is too noble an ideal to be thrown as a cloak around those ideologies that seek to destroy it, to hide their tawdriness by its bright glory. Communism is laughing up its sleeve at us today hoping that we will continue to thus cheapen freedom with this definition. They know that our continuing to do so will be their means of infiltrating and upsetting our way of life.

What happens to the ideal of freedom, if freedom of speech is interpreted to mean that a man can say exactly what he wants to say, regardless of the consequences to others? That gives one man the same right to falsehood as another man has to truth. If this were to become a common interpretation, before long there would be no such thing as integrity in our nation.

What happens to the ideal of freedom if freedom of the press is interpreted to mean that one can put into print anything he desires to write about another man? This would give him the right to write falsely and thus destroy another's character.

What happens to the ideal of freedom if freedom of property rights is interpreted to mean that every man is free to acquire what he wants? If this were the common interpretation, then one man would have the right to take another man's property, without interference from any person or power.

What happens to the ideal of freedom if freedom of worship is interpreted to mean what Roger Williams said it meant—that a man is free to worship or not to worship? If this were the common interpretation, we would be a nation of irreligious men before long.

What happens to the ideal of freedom, if freedom of the ballot is interpreted to mean that a man is free to vote or not to vote, as he sees fit? If this became the common interpretation and all men saw fit not to vote, then before long we would be going to the polls at the point of a gun, to vote for only one man in each office.

The notion that freedom is a right, with no relationship to duty, is a false idea. Freedom is a right, but it is also a responsibility. We misuse our freedom when we use it as a selfish ideal to gain what we want with no regard for the other fellow. As Paul reminded the Christians of Galatia, so he reminds us, "For you were called to freedom, brethren; only do not use your freedom as an opportunity for the flesh, but through love be servants of one another." (Galatians 5:13.) Is Paul not saying that while freedom is a right— "you were called to freedom, brethren"—it is also a tremendous responsibility?

The fact that we are free to worship and choose our religion places us under a great responsibility. We are under responsibility to those who through the ages have given of their lifeblood that this freedom might be kept alive. Men have gone to the guillotine because they chose to worship according to the dictates of their own consciences. Men of the past have been martyrs rather than relinquish this God-given right. If we fail to take advantage of this freedom today, then those men, as far as we are concerned, died in vain. But then, we have another responsibility where freedom of worship is concerned; we have a responsibility to every person who lives today and to every person who will be born tomorrow. If we are lethargic in our duty to God and his church today, then we are hastening the day when freedom of worship will no longer be a reality for anyone. By our indifference we are casting the only vote we have to cast, that the doors of the churches be closed and man be denied the privilege of worshiping and choosing his religion. We are making it possible for paganism or dialectical materialism to become the religion of America.

The fact that we enjoy freedom of speech places us under an important responsibility. Again we are under responsibility to those who have fought in all the wars of the ages to guarantee this inalienable right to all of God's children. If we misuse this freedom, then the men who have died to make this freedom possible died in vain. But we are under a more important responsibility. The fact that we enjoy freedom of speech places us under the responsibility to speak the truth. Jesus was saying the same thing when he said, "You will know the truth, and the truth will make you free." (John 8:32.) Falsehood entangles us and others in the yoke of bondage.

The fact that we enjoy the freedom of the ballot places us under a vital responsibility. Again we are under responsibility to those who have gone before us and paved the highway of life with this freedom. Those men who left their footprints in the snow at Valley Forge paid a high price for the democratic principles that we enjoy as American citizens.

They fought that we might not grow up under the tyranny of an unjust king; but that we might live in a country whose government exists only by the consent of the governed.

On February 22, 1952, George Washington's birthday, the writer stood at attention at a flag-raising ceremony at Valley Forge. It was a moment of high emotion, as in his mind's eye he saw that rugged band of troops under the generalship of George Washington suffering for his right to cast a vote in a general election. If we do not exercise this right, to vote and vote intelligently, those men died in vain. It seemed to the writer that he could hear them saying in one grand chorus, "Don't let us down. Use the freedom that we bought at the price of our lives." We are under responsibility to them. We are, however, under another responsibility where the freedom of the ballot is concerned. We are under responsibility to every citizen of America and every future citizen of America. If we fail to exercise our right to vote, and to vote intelligently, we are casting a negative vote against the democratic system of free elections. We are placing every other citizen and future citizen in jeopardy. We are endangering American freedom.

The fact that we enjoy freedom of choice of profession and occupation, which carries with it the freedom of education and preparation for that profession, freedom to acquire, possess and inherit property; freedom in the establishment and maintenance of free enterprise and the possession and enjoyment of the fruits of our labors, which means freedom from want, places us under a grave responsibility. Paul said this when he said, "Only do not use your freedom as an opportunity for the flesh, but through love be servants of one another." (Galatians 5:13.) In answer to the question, "Am I my brother's keeper?" the answer should be, "No, I am my brother's brother."

We do not have to look far today to see that these rights are not available to all of God's children. Some citizens of America do not have equal opportunity of choice of profession and occupation because they do not have equal opportunities of education and of employment. Unless we are as willing to guarantee these inalienable rights to others as we are to demand them for ourselves, then we do not deserve them for ourselves. And these are things that cannot be legislated. If we, as Christian citizens of America, stand by and make it necessary for government to legislate human rights and civil liberties, we are falling far short of Paul's admonition when he said, "by love serve one another."

What is freedom? Any definition of it will be like the score of a sonata with no musician to play it. Liberty has been defined as "self-regulated obedience to self-recognized law." It is the happy, creative, victorious reconciliation of necessity and impulse. There is no true freedom except freedom in restraint. Our freedom to get what we want must be under the restraint of not depriving someone else of what he has the right to want.

The writer once heard a great pianist give a concert. Within five minutes the beauty of the music brought tears of joy to his eyes. The music was so free it filled the great concert hall with tenderness and sweetness. While the music was free, the musician was under great restraint. He was under the restraint of space. He had to confine his playing to the keyboard of the grand piano. But he was under another kind of restraint; behind the sonata of Mozart and Beethoven were years of disciplined study and practice. He had made himself a slave to his art that the music might be freed.

Freedom can evoke such music as this from the orchestration of life if we will only obey the admonition of Paul, "Through love be servants of one another." (Galatians 5:13.) If our definition of freedom is self-regulated obedience to self-recognized law; if the freedom we practice is a victorious reconciliation of necessity and impulse; if the freedom we prize is freedom in restraint, then our very lives will sing, "Let freedom ring."

Let freedom ring!—in America and throughout the world.

Date Due

Code 4386-04, CLS-4, Broadman Supplies, Nashville, Tenn., Printed in U.S.A.